Dogs at Work:

Make Every Day Take Your Dog to Work Day!

By Mary DiTosto

Dedication

This book is dedicated to all of the wonderful employers
[like mine :)] who are kind-hearted enough to allow
canine companions at work.

Table of Contents

Author's Note

To make things easier for me, the author, I will sometimes refer to a general place of work as an office throughout the book. It's an easy, generic term. I understand that your work situation may look nothing like an office and there are countless other locations where you may want to bring your dog. Whether you work in an office, automotive garage, or plant nursery, etc. these tips are meant to be as generic as possible to be useful in as many various workplace situations as possible.

When my dog, Sadie, was just three months old, she began accompanying me to work every day. In the beginning, she spent her time napping and playing in a doggy playpen. We were still working on obedience training and housebreaking at that time, so she needed to prove her mastery of those concepts before she could have more freedom. Fairly quickly, Sadie became used to the office environment. She began to understand that there were some different rules at work and at home. Not everything in the office was okay to touch. Sometimes the humans would be too busy to play. Keeping quiet was very important, no matter what weird sounds were heard nearby. Sadie became content to nap on her bed while the humans worked and enjoyed their attention whenever someone took a break.

Sadie is now seven years old and still enjoys coming to work with me every day. She is excited every time we reach the office parking lot. Sadie immediately greets everyone in the office and is noticeably disappointed if someone is not at work. She checks the place over to make sure everything is as it should be. She supervises the filling of her water dish. Then she is happy to nap until she is offered a snack and lunch. This routine Sadie and I have created works very well for both of us. Every day she does some silly or adorable action that brightens what might be a boring work day. Not a day goes by that I'm not thankful for the constant companionship of my faithful pup at home and especially at work.

<u>Introduction</u>

There is a growing trend around the world involving more and more workplaces becoming dog friendly. In recent years, there has been a dramatic increase in the number of workplaces that allow dogs. Employers are beginning to understand the benefits of stress reduction and increased productivity that are the result of happier employees. And nothing makes a pet parent happier than the company of their favorite canine companion. Dogs increase creativity, compassion and morale in general, which in turn increases productivity.

When you think about benefits like increased morale and boosts to productivity, then of course it's a great idea to bring any dog to any workplace, right? Well, before you go any further with the idea of bringing your dog with you to work, you must ask yourself the following two questions:

Is your dog appropriate for a workplace environment?

Think about your dog's temperament.
Is your dog friendly and comfortable with strangers?
Is your dog friendly and comfortable with other dogs?
Does your dog have trouble with food aggression?
Is your dog too high energy to behave calmly through the work day?
Does he or she have a good grasp of basic obedience commands and behaviors?
Does your dog bark excessively?
Make sure that your decision to bring your dog to work will benefit both of you. A dog that is unhappy or uncomfortable in their environment is more likely to misbehave.

Is your workplace an appropriate environment for your dog?

Priority number one is your dog's health and safety. Are there aspects of your workplace that would be dangerous for your dog? Are there extremely loud noises? Chemicals? Toxins?
Is the temperature uncomfortably hot for someone that permanently wears a fur coat?
Are there too many stairs for your dog to handle?
Are the floors too slippery for your dog to walk safely?

Have a discussion with your boss about the idea of bringing your dog into work. Make sure you are fully aware of all the rules, regulations, and policies in your workplace. For example, there may be areas like a cafeteria or break room where dogs are prohibited. You may need to provide health or vaccination records to your company before a dog is allowed on the premises. Do not be surprised if there are other paperwork requirements like a liability waiver.

When you're considering a change to the everyday routine in your and your dog's lives, it's always a good idea to think about the change from every angle. Change can bring about both positive and negative results. As the decision maker, you must ensure a positive result to the best of your ability. A helpful tool in visualizing the positives and negatives of your decision is a pros and cons list.

Below is an example of a pros and cons list about bringing your dog to work with you:

Pros:

- More opportunities for quality bonding time every day
- A dog provides a morale boost for you and your coworkers.
- If work becomes stressful, you can take a quick break to pet your dog and release the tension. Even if your dog is not technically an emotional support animal, he or she will still provide comfort and stress relief to those who need it.
- Enriching for your dog to explore a new environment with new sights and smells
- Beneficial for your health as you have to get up and move around more often to tend to your dog's needs
- Beneficial for your dog's health as he or she will now be active during the hours that were usually spent sleeping alone
- You won't spend your workday worrying about what your dog is doing alone at home.
- Your dog won't have the chance to get in trouble or make a mess while unsupervised at home.
- You won't need to spend money on doggy daycare or a dog walker if your dog is with you all day.

Cons:

- Your dog may distract you from your work.
- Your dog may make the occasional mistake or mess you will need to clean up.
- You will probably have to deal with shedding and fur around your workplace.
- You may have to deal with barking or other similar disruptive behaviors.
- You will have to interrupt your work day to take your dog out for bathroom breaks.
- Your workplace may become cluttered with your dog's belongings.
- Your dog may become too attached to your presence nearby, finding it more difficult to be left home alone.
- You may experience the displeasure of non-animal-loving coworkers.

As you can see, the pros definitely outweigh the cons on this list. You may want to create your own, more detailed list that pertains to the specifics of your particular workplace. Hopefully your own pros and cons list will just as clearly show that regardless of the minor inconveniences, having your dog keep you company at work will make life better overall.

Once your decision to bring your dog to work has been made, you need to think about the necessary preparations. This book provides you with the tips and advice you need to successfully integrate your dog into your work environment.

Getting Ready

    Before your dog ever makes an appearance at work, you need to make sure to get your workplace prepared for your dog. In this section of the book, you will find advice on a wide range of topics that need to be considered in preparation for your dog's workplace arrival. At the end of this book there is also a helpful checklist of items that will help you make sure you have everything you can need or want when your pup is at work with you.

Make sure your workplace is aware that you have a dog on the premises.

    "Beware of Dog" signs have been a common part of life since ancient times. It's a polite way of informing visitors that a dog is on the premises. You need to give the visitors of your workplace that same courtesy of an advanced warning. Place a clearly visible sign near the workplace entrance stating that there is a dog inside. If the classic beware of dog signs feels too off-putting for you or your employer, consider alternatives like a cute welcome mat or even a printed sign with your dog's picture saying he or she is waiting to welcome visitors inside.

If you have an office where your dog will spend most of their time, then a sign for that particular door would be helpful as well. Consider a sign similar to those on hotel room doors - something double sided that you can change to display the appropriate message. On one side indicate your dog is inside. On the other, indicate your dog is not in the office at the moment. These signs will warn your coworkers of the situation behind your closed door. They will know to be careful opening the door if your dog is inside and will not be startled by any canine greetings.

I would also recommend one of the official pet rescue emergency window signs. These signs alert first responders that a pet is on the premises in case of emergency. You write on the sign the number and type of pet you have inside and then firefighters know what to look for in an evacuation.

Make sure the floor is as dog proof as can be.

Encourage others to keep food, office supplies, or personal items off of the floor whenever possible. Check any plants in your workplace to make sure that they aren't poisonous to dogs. Even if a plant is too high up for your dog to reach, leaves or petals may fall to the floor. Also check for any gum at your dog's level. Most people don't realize that many brands If gum contain the ingredient xylitol, which is toxic to dogs.

Designate a dog sitter.

Ask your coworkers for a volunteer to watch your dog if you need to step out of the office for a short period of time. Choose someone who will check on your pup, keep your dog company, or possibly feed or walk him/her, if you need to be gone for longer than expected.

Dog food

Dry food is the best option for dog food in a workplace environment. It's far easier to handle, store, and clean up than wet food. Consider bringing the amount of dry food your dog should have for the week at one time. This way if you're running late one day, you won't have to worry about getting your dog's food ready. But you also don't want to store too much food at work because it will likely become stale before your dog has a chance to eat all of it. In an effort to keep the food as fresh as possible, store the kibble in an airtight food storage container. This will also ensure that the food does not attract any bugs or rodents into your workspace. For the same reason, make sure you do not leave any food out overnight. Aside from potentially attracting pests with unattended bowls of food, you may also attract other dogs from around your workplace. Since other dogs may be on different foods or have dietary restrictions, you can't leave your dog's food unattended without facing the possible consequences of upset tummies and upset dog owners.

If your dog eats only canned or wet food, you will probably need to investigate refrigeration options to keep the dog food fresh. You may choose to keep a cooler or small refrigerator by your workspace. Or if there is a break room or kitchen with a shared refrigerator, consider keeping the can or container of dog food in a lunch box or bag within the fridge. There may be others sharing the kitchen with you that won't like the idea of dog food sitting right next to their human food. It may seem like a silly way of thinking, but it's better to be overly considerate of other people's feelings while at work.

Water

Water is an obvious necessity for your dog, but something you may not typically think about while at work. Maybe you bring your own coffee with you every morning, followed by whatever you choose to drink when out to lunch. But your dog needs access to fresh water throughout the day, not just at meal time. Is the water from the bathroom sink your best option for filling your dog's water bowl? Is there a water fountain in the building? If there is a water cooler, break room, or kitchen where access to fresh water will not be a problem? Regardless, you may want to keep a few bottles of water with the rest of your dog supplies, just in case.

Bowls

Obviously you will need to provide your dog with both a food and a water bowl. While any old bowl can get the job done, it may be worth considering certain types of bowls that can make your life easier. For instance, collapsible bowls come in handy for on-the-go activities. You can easily grab a collapsible bowl or two to bring with you for spontaneous lunches outdoors. It's also easy to transport collapsible bowls back and forth from home for thorough cleanings when necessary. You may also want to think about bowls in terms of stability. Your dog has less of a chance of making a mess when their bowls are too sturdy to be knocked over. You can also consider bowls that sit in frame.

It may also be worthwhile to consider a slow feeder bowl. For those of you unfamiliar with the concept, a slow feeder bowl has ridges and grooves at the bottom to make the food harder for your dog to obtain. This makes your dog slow down the eating process, requiring smaller bites and more focused attention. In a workplace environment, longer mealtimes keep your dog entertained longer, focusing his or her attention on the mental challenge of extracting all the food from the slow feeder bowl.

Placemat

Consider placing your dog's food and water bowls on a placemat. There are many types available at pet stores made specifically to handle pet messes. A placemat will protect the floor of your workspace from any accidental spills. I'm sure you're aware of just how messy your dog can be when eating and drinking. A placemat can make cleaning up at the end of the day much easier.

Treats

Similar to food, consider portioning out treats for a week at a time. Keep treats in air tight containers out of your dog's reach. Choose longer lasting treats that are useful for keeping your dog entertained and distracted. Also keep on hand tiny treats or treats that can be easily broken into small pieces for rewards throughout the day. You should also consider giving your dog a breath freshening treat while at work. Your dog will enjoy the treat and your coworkers will appreciate the lack of doggy breath.

Chews

You may need to provide your dog with safe items for chewing. If your dog tries to chew or bite on objects in your workplace, be prepared to offer your dog a safe, dog appropriate item to chew. Options include non-edible bone toys like those made by Nylabone or bully sticks. Personally I don't recommend rawhide to chew on since many dogs have difficulty digesting that material.

Beds

Your dog needs at least one or more comfortable places to lie down. Most likely your dog will spend the majority of the work day napping in the location you provide. Make sure the bed is placed in a safe area, out of the way, but still within eyesight. Choose a bed your dog is unlikely to destroy/shred/chew on. Consider a bed that you can spot clean if it gets dirty or maybe one with a removable cover you can take home to wash.

Toys

First and foremost, you don't want to give your dog toys that will make a lot of noise or disrupt the work day. If your dog strongly prefers toys that squeak, consider trying an ultrasonic squeaker toy. These specially made toys have a squeaker that works at a frequency only dogs can hear. You won't have to worry about bothering coworkers or trying to be heard over squeaking noises with these particular toys. Just keep in mind that other dogs in your workplace will be able to hear the squeaking, so don't be surprised if another dog shows up to play.

A great option for quiet, engaged play are treat dispensing toys and puzzles. There are a large variety of shapes, sizes, and difficulty levels available at pet stores. These toys can be filled with small treats or kibble and will keep your dog entertained for extended periods of time trying to work out the mechanism to release the treats or kibble. You can fill a toy with your dog's lunch portion of dry food and your dog can happily play while eating lunch at the same time.

Plan for bathroom breaks.

Scout out areas of grass or other places nearby where your dog can do his or her business during the workday. If you have your own office, you may want to consider laying down a potty pad, just in case of emergencies. You should also leave a stash of potty pads in the bathroom. That way if your dog has to go and you don't have time to take him or her all the way outside, your dog can do their business on a pad in the proper location. Then you can dispose of the pad just like a sanitary napkin. This is also a possible solution to take care of your dog's needs during inclement weather. Potty pads are also useful to mop up any spills caused by your dog (or caused by someone accidentally knocking over your dog's water).

Cleaning supplies

Keep the necessary cleaning supplies on hand, just in case. If possible, choose organic, dog-safe products. Disinfectant wipes are an absolute must. Pet stain remover is also useful, but hopefully you will never need to use it. Paper towels are another must have cleaning product.

Should you bring in a dog crate?

Is your dog crate trained? If the answer is yes, consider bringing a portable crate with you to work. Your dog will have an automatic safe place to sleep and retreat to if he or she feels overwhelmed by the unfamiliar surroundings. A crate is also an extremely useful tool to keep your dog safely contained if you need to step away from your desk for a meeting or other short errand.

When placing your dog's crate, choose a spot that is in your line of sight but out of the path of foot traffic. You don't want anyone accidentally banging into the crate and hurting themselves or your dog. You also want to make sure the temperature is appropriate in the area you place the crate. Lastly, make sure you bring a blanket or other item you can use to cover the crate. The darkness will encourage your dog to sleep and stay quiet in the cave-like atmosphere.

Would a baby gate be useful?

If you have your own office with a door, consider utilizing a baby gate. You can leave your door open so your dog can watch the comings and goings of your workplace without getting in anyone's way. There are even some walk-through models where you can easily swing a section of the gate open instead of having to step over it.

Have poop bags handy.

Keep poop bags readily available in your workspace. You can never have too many poop bags. Your coworkers may need some for their own pets. They also come in handy as small garbage bags if you have a small mess needing to be contained.

Keep some hand sanitizer easily accessible.

Clean hands are always a good idea. If you've been handling all kinds of items during the work day, you may want to sanitize your hands before feeding your dog. Similarly, you may want to sanitize your hands after dealing with dog food before going back to work. And some coworkers may appreciate the offer of some hand sanitizer after petting or playing with your dog.

Bring a lint roller.

Keep a lint roller in your desk in case you need it. It's always a good idea to look presentable at work, including removing excess fur from your clothing. It's also a nice gesture to offer the use of a lint roller to coworkers when necessary, especially if your dog has shed directly onto them.

Consider the flooring in your workplace.

Some dogs have trouble walking on floors that are too slippery. Some dogs may be too cold or uncomfortable with cement floors. Some dogs are even afraid to step on new or unusual types of flooring. Most flooring concerns can be solved by giving your dog a comfortable bed to sleep on. However, it may also add to your dog's comfort to bring in one or more area rugs, runners, or even welcome mats.

There are quite a few benefits to having a rug for your dog in your workspace. Besides providing a softer place to lay down, it also gives your dog a specific area for all their activities. If your dog makes a mess or the rug gets dirty, you can bring it home to clean or replace without worrying about damaging your workplace. The texture of the rug will give your dog sure footing, which he or she may not find in other areas of your workplace. Your dog will be safer from foot traffic and chair traffic if everyone knows he or she hangs out on that specific rug.

Establish a drawer / shelf / box for your dog's belongings.

You don't want to leave dog toys or bowls on the floor overnight in case cleaning needs to be done. If you have a designated spot for everything your dog needs, it's easy to remember to put everything back and notice if anything is missing. If you need to access something in a hurry, you'll be glad that whatever you need can be found quickly in your dog drawer / box / shelf.

Consider a portable playpen.

If you have a puppy or smaller dog, a dog playpen is a great tool to have in your workplace. Your dog will be safe and contained, but still nearby and able to move around more than in a crate. Also a playpen will keep all of your dog's things contained as well so that you don't have to worry about someone accidentally stepping on a dog toy or chew.

Is your dog's veterinarian near your workplace?

If your usual vet is too far away, make sure you know the address and phone number of the closest veterinarian and emergency clinic, just in case. You should also keep a business card or note in a prominent place with the vet's contact information. Hopefully it will never be needed, but in case you have to go out and leave your dog behind, your coworkers will have access to the information in an emergency.

Make sure your coworkers are aware of what foods are harmful to dogs.

Most people are aware of the dangers of chocolate for dogs. But non-dog owners may not realize that grapes, for example, can be equally as harmful. Put a list of foods that are hazardous to dogs on your office refrigerator or in some other common area. You don't want a coworker unknowingly giving your dog a dangerous snack. Be sure to include any known food allergies your dog may have on the list.

Keep some towels or napkins near the entrance to your workplace.

If it's a snowy or rainy day, you'll need to wipe your dog's paws so that he or she isn't making a mess all over the place. Yes, your coworkers' shoes are just as likely to make a mess, but you don't want to give anyone a reason to be annoyed with your dog.

<u>Make sure some, if not all, of your dog's
belongings are in place before you bring your dog
into the space for the first time.</u>

Having everything set up from day one will ensure
that your dog doesn't get confused about where he or she
belongs in your workplace. Familiar toys or bedding will
also provide immediate comfort for your dog in an
unfamiliar place. When everything around them smells
new and different, your dog will gravitate toward the
items that smell like home.

Preparing Your Pup

The first step to bringing your dog to work with you is familiarizing your dog with the workplace itself. Bring your dog to work for the first time at night, on a weekend, or at some other quiet time. That way your dog can sniff and explore and get used to the space without too much activity or overwhelming distractions. Use small pieces of healthy treats to create positive associations as your dog progresses through your workplace.

Before entering the door of your workplace, have your dog sit for a moment.

This will help bring your dog's excitement level down and prepare him or her to enter the work environment more calmly and peacefully. If you allow your dog into your workplace in an excited fashion, he or she is more likely to create a disruption, possibly by barking excitedly or jumping on coworkers or customers. Giving your dog the sit command before you open the door allows your dog to focus on you instead of the potential excitement on the other side of that door. Depending on your dog's level of excitement, you may need to keep your dog in a sit position for a longer period of time until he or she becomes calm. Then, once your dog is calm and relaxed, you can open the door and head inside.

Remember to always walk through the door before your dog.

     This serves two purposes. From a psychology standpoint, you entering first reinforces your superior position. You are in charge and your dog must follow. From a more practical point of view, entering the door first allows you a quick overview of your surroundings. When entering a public place, you never know what you are going to encounter. By going in first, you can recognize any potential hazards or problems and react accordingly. For example, someone may be carrying a large box towards the door and if your dog ran ahead of you, both your dog and that person could become injured. If you always enter first through a doorway, you will have much better control over the situation.

Teach your dog a work boundary.

     Spend some time with your dog on a leash showing him or her their limits within your workplace. If your dog tries to go beyond a set boundary, use the leash to stop forward momentum. Tell your dog "No", he or she can't go that way. After a few repetitions, your dog should begin to understand the invisible boundary lines. Just remember that no training is foolproof and it is always safest to keep an eye on your dog. You never know when some sudden sound or enticing smell will make your dog forget all of the rules.

     Boundary training is especially useful if there is a door that's always being opened and closed. Your dog needs to know not to go past that point without you. You can't have your dog dashing out of the door at every opportunity.

Reinforce / Teach the No Command.

Most dogs are probably very familiar with the word No. Before entering a work environment, make sure that your dog understands that No means that whatever they were just doing is unacceptable. It is also very useful as a preventative command. If your dog begins sniffing around a garbage can, the No command will tell your dog not to interact with the garbage can. Or maybe your dog has jumped onto a chair where he or she is not allowed. The No command tells your dog that sitting on that chair is not acceptable behavior.

Reinforce / Teach the Leave It Command.

The Leave It command is a more specific form of the No command, where you tell your dog he or she is not allowed to touch certain objects, even if they are within reach. This command is useful in your everyday life with your dog as you never know when something harmful may accidentally be within your dog's reach. A good time to practice this command is while out for walks. Your dog will inevitably want to sniff something he or she encounters on the walk. Allow your dog to sniff the object for a moment, then give the Leave It command and resume walking. If your dog attempts to touch or lick or pick up the object, add the No command along with saying Leave It. After some repetition, your dog will begin to understand that

Leave It means he or she can smell something but not touch it.

Familiarize your dog with common workplace items.

When a puppy is exploring their environment, they often use their mouth to get to know new objects. Most dogs grow out of this behavior with the help of obedience training, but sometimes new sights and smells are too tempting to ignore. However, if you expose your dog to items he or she might encounter at your workplace, they will be less likely to lick / bite / chew / steal / eat those items if they are within your dog's reach at work.

In preparation for bringing your dog to work with you, try incorporating common items from your workplace into his or her training. For example, if you work in an office, place items like a stapler, pens, paper clips, etc. on the floor. Allow your dog to sniff and examine the objects, but give the Leave It command before your dog actually touches anything.

Reinforce / Teach the Drop It Command.

Even the most well behaved dogs can be sneaky sometimes and pick up an object they shouldn't have. But with the Drop It command, your dog should know to put down an item immediately. You may need to point to the ground or hold out your hand to reinforce the message that your dog needs to relinquish the item he or she is holding. You may get those sad puppy dog eyes for ending your dog's fun. But you need to be firm with the Drop It command, maintaining your focus and eye contact with your dog until the item is released. Do not try to pull on the item to take it away. That will only begin a game of tug of war. Your dog needs to release the item all on their own in order for the Drop It command to be a success.

It is especially important in a work environment for your dog to have a reliable Drop It command. You never know what items your coworkers may accidentally leave within your dog's reach.

Reinforce / Teach the Come Command.

Come is probably one of the first commands your dog ever learned. Your dog may be an expert with the Come command in your house or backyard. But in a busy workplace with lots of people and excitement, your dog may become too distracted to promptly obey. That's why it is a good idea to reinforce the Come command before bringing your dog to work.

A great place to work on this command is the dog park. Dog parks are usually busy places, away from home, with exciting smells and sounds. Your dog will probably be distracted, similar to the distractions of a busy workplace. But in the dog park, your dog will be in a securely fenced in area, able to roam freely, giving you the opportunity to practice the Come command.

Reinforce / Teach the Stay Command.

Of all the commands your dog learned as a puppy, the Stay command is probably the one you use the least. At home your dog can probably roam freely without being told to Stay. Away from home, your dog is probably on a leash at all times, making the use of the Stay command unnecessary. But at work, Stay can be a very useful command for you and your dog. Your dog may be anxious at the idea of you leaving him or her in the unfamiliar setting of your workplace, and thus may ignore your Stay commands at first. Repetition and reinforcement, with plenty of praise and treats of course, will help your dog realize that Stay means Stay, no matter where you are.

Reinforce / Teach the Quiet Command.

Whether you use the word Quiet or Shush or even Zip It, it is critically important for your dog to master the concept of silence in your workplace. Most dogs can't help but bark if there is an unexpected loud noise or strange sound. That's why you must prepare your dog with a Quiet command to stop the barking immediately. At my own workplace, we have had great success telling my dog that she needs to "use her office voice." This phrase reminds my dog that barking is not allowed in the workplace and she needs to stay calm and quiet in that location.

To begin training a Quiet command, you must first find something at home that typically causes your dog to bark, like the doorbell. Set off the doorbell so that your dog starts barking. Then issue the Quiet command. If your dog immediately stops barking, praise your dog enthusiastically saying "Yes! Good Quiet!" and repeat the exercise to reinforce the command.

However, most dogs will probably not stop barking the first time you say the command. You will most likely need to combine the command with another action that gets your dog to momentarily focus attention on you, which should stop the barking. For instance, you can try saying "Quiet" and loudly clapping your hands to get your dog's attention. Similarly you could try stomping your foot or waving your hands in the air, or any type of sudden gesture that will break your dog's focus on the cause of the barking.

Be careful not to repeatedly shout "Quiet" attempting to be louder than the sound of the barking. This will only make your dog bark more excitedly. Your command must be said calmly and firmly only once. If your dog doesn't respond, walk away and try it again a minute or two later. You may need to move directly into your dog's line of sight to better maintain his or her attention while beginning to learn this command.

Reinforce / Teach the Place Command.

The Place Command tells your dog to go to a designated spot right away. This command is very useful in ensuring that your dog is out of the way, in their proper place, when necessary. Of course the first step is to determine the right location for your dog's place. An ideal spot would be away from doorways and foot traffic, preferably within your line of sight. Once you select the location, your dog's bed or crate or other comfort items should be placed there.

When you are ready to introduce your dog to his or her place, start off with your dog on a leash. Walk your dog on the leash toward the area, telling him or her to "Go to your Place." Once your dog sits or lies down on the designated spot, praise your dog saying "Yes! Good Place!" Repeat this exercise on leash a few times before removing the guiding influence of the leash. Before long, all it should take is a finger pointed in the right direction with the words "Go to your Place" and your dog will settle down comfortably in his or her spot.

Keep your dog well-groomed and clean in your work environment.

Comb / brush / groom / bathe your dog often to keep the office environment as clean and fur free as possible. Obviously shedding is inevitable for most dog breeds, but more frequent brushing will help remove the excess fur in a neater fashion. Try to dry your dog whenever possible so he or she doesn't leave wet footprints all around your workplace. Clean off any dirt or mud before entering. As a dog owner you probably know you also need to make sure your dog's hind end is clean after bathroom breaks. You don't want to carpet or office furniture being used as doggy toilet paper. You may also want to try doggy dry shampoo or conditioning spray to keep your dog smelling fresh and looking neat between baths.

Teach your dog chair etiquette.

Make sure your dog is aware that rolling chairs can be dangerous. I'm sure you're used to looking down to make sure your dog is out of the way before making sudden movements. But if your coworker doesn't have any pets, he or she may not think to check if your dog is in the way before rolling their chair back.

Familiarize your dog with workplace noises.

Spend some time desensitizing your dog to noises that are common in your workplace. Since a dog's ears are much more sensitive than a human's ears, noises that may not bother you at work may be difficult for your dog. In an already unfamiliar environment, sudden or loud noises may cause your dog to feel stress or anxiety. This is why it can be beneficial for your dog to acclimatize to the sounds common to your workplace as soon as possible.

For instance there may be multiple phones ringing or printers that suddenly start printing, startling your dog. Knocking or doorbells could cause your dog to bark. Loud machinery, heating or air conditioning may take some getting used to.

Does your dog have a microchip?

If your dog does not have a microchip, you should seriously discuss the possibility with your veterinarian. A microchip is a safe, inexpensive, and permanent way to make sure your dog has a form of identification. Your veterinarian implants the grain of rice sized chip using a needle in a five second procedure, similar to most vaccinations. Once implanted, the microchip contains a permanent identification number that can be read by a scanner at any animal care facility. That identification number is then matched in a database to your name and phone number, showing that the dog with that microchip belongs to you.

If your dog already has a microchip, make sure your contact information is correct with the microchip company. If your dog is lost and your phone number and address in the microchip database is out of date, no one will be able to inform you if your dog is found.

Make sure your dog knows not to jump.

In a workplace environment, your dog should not be allowed to jump up onto people or objects uninvited. You cannot take the chance of your dog accidentally knocking someone over or scratching someone or damaging their clothing. If your dog likes to jump excitedly while greeting people, you may need to keep your dog on a leash. On a leash, you can control how closely your dog can approach other people, ensuring he or she can't jump up. For people who would like to interact with your dog, instruct them to ignore your dog if he or she becomes too excited and starts jumping. Once your dog has calmed down, then they can be given affection and attention.

Make sure your dog doesn't relentlessly beg for food.

It is inevitable that someone in your workplace will have some food or drinks. You must make sure that your dog does not immediately go begging every time he or she smells food. This problem can be eased by feeding your dog at an earlier time so he or she may not be as interested in other's food. Liberal use of the No command may also be necessary to keep this problem at bay.

Make sure your coworkers know your rules about giving food to your dog.

Many pet parents feel differently about what, where, and when their dog can eat. You should always ask permission before feeding something to someone else's dog. Conversely, you should establish with your coworkers what is and is not allowed in terms of feeding your dog.

If you allow your coworkers to share a bite of something with your dog, insist they place the piece of food into your dog's bowl. That way your dog knows that the only food he or she is allowed to eat comes out of that bowl.

Make sure your dog knows not to steal or chew on shoes / slippers.

You may think that your dog is too old or well behaved for such juvenile behavior as stealing or chewing on shoes. But a new environment with exciting new smells can sometimes cause your dog to act in surprising ways. And many people change shoes, wear slippers, or even take off their shoes at work, leaving tempting pieces of footwear sitting unattended at eye level with your dog.

Keep your dog away from garbage cans.

Make sure to use the "No" command anytime your dog so much as sniffs a garbage can. There may be delicious food smells your dog can't resist, causing all kinds of mess and trouble if your dog overturns the trash can. But worse than a mess, there could be dangerous items within that trash that could harm your dog.

Plan a neutral introduction to other office dogs.

If there are other dogs at your workplace, plan a meet and greet for all the dogs somewhere outdoors. Try going on walks together or take an office-wide trip to the dog park so that the dogs can get to know each other in neutral territory. This will hopefully prevent the dogs from becoming territorial in your workplace.

Keep your dog up-to-date on all vaccinations and preventative treatments.

While your workplace should require all dogs on the premises to have all the proper vaccinations, you can really only be certain about your own dog. Make sure to visit your veterinarian regularly for your dog to receive the recommended vaccinations to keep your pet as healthy as possible. Remember to use the monthly / quarterly flea / tick / heartworm preventatives your vet recommends for your area. This way if a coworker's new puppy or rescue dog turns out to have fleas or kennel cough, your dog will be as protected as possible.

It's also recommended that your dog be spayed or neutered before entering a workplace environment. Along with the obvious benefit of no unplanned puppies, spayed and neutered dogs are typically calmer and better behaved. There is less need for embarrassing humping behaviors and less mess without marking and heat cycles. And the most important benefit of all is the significant reduction in reproductive cancers, meaning that spayed and neutered dogs statistically live longer lives.

Day-to-Day Advice

When your dog finally begins joining you at work on a regular basis, you will establish a comfortable routine of day-to-day activities. However, as a dog owner, you know that dogs can be unpredictable. Sometimes they do funny, spontaneous things that make us humans smile and love them even more. But other times that spontaneous behavior can cause some trouble. You need to be prepared to handle whatever comes your way quickly and efficiently, causing as little disruption to your workplace as possible. In simple terms, with a dog by your side you need to expect the unexpected.

Make sure your dog wears his or her collar with up-to-date tags while in your workplace at all times.

Does your dog's ID tag have your cell phone number on it? If the tag only has your home address or landline phone number, it could cause some confusion and delay in the return of your dog should the worst happen and he or she gets lost at work. You may want to have an ID tag made with your workplace address and phone number on it so that if your dog is found in your work neighborhood, he or she can be quickly returned to the right place.

Remove tag silencers from your dog's collar.

At home, tag silencers are great for getting rid of that annoying jingling noise your dog's collar makes with every little movement. But in a workplace environment, that noise can prove very useful in keeping track of your dog. You may think the noise of your dog's tags rattling would be distracting at work, but the noise will actually help keep your dog safe by alerting your coworkers that your dog is nearby.

Provide your coworkers with healthy treats to give your dog when interacting.

You want to make sure that your coworkers do not feed your dog too many treats. By handing out a reasonable amount, you can control what your dog may receive. And with coworkers giving your dog the occasional treat, your dog will build up positive associations with those people and become more relaxed with the people in his or her environment.

Keep small treats in your pocket to reward and reinforce behaviors.

Dogs need immediate positive or negative feedback to understand what actions are good or bad. If you need to look in a drawer or go to another room to find a treat for your dog, it will take too long for your dog to understand the treat is a reward. Of course your dog will always happily accept a treat, but he or she won't associate that treat as a reward for a correct action unless the reward is delivered immediately.

Consider feeding your dog his or her lunch right before lunch time for the humans.

If you typically feed your dog only twice a day, consider adding a third meal on workdays. Feed your dog half of his or her normal portion of dog food for breakfast in the morning. Then, right before lunch time, feed your dog the other half of his or her meal. That way your dog will be satisfied and less likely to beg for other people's lunch.

Lunch time is the perfect time for a walk.

Consider walking to the park to eat your lunch or maybe walking with your dog to a food truck or street vendor and eating al fresco. Your dog will enjoy the exercise and change of scenery, as well as the opportunity to take care of business. When you return to work, your dog should be more likely to nap after the excitement of fresh air and exercise.

Spend a few minutes with your dog every hour.

Experts say that it's better for your health if you step away from your desk for at least five minutes every hour.

So use those five minutes for quality dog time. Take your pup for a potty break. Do a five minute training session. Wow your coworkers with a little demonstration of your dog's favorite tricks. With those little breaks to look forward to, your day will pass quickly alongside your pup.

Be prepared for your dog to act in unexpected or atypical ways.

Although your dog may be very well behaved at home, don't be surprised if he or she starts acting like a naughty puppy at work. Your dog may revert to bad behavior because he or she is unsure of their new environment. Be patient with your dog's mistakes and use positive reinforcement to remind him or her of the correct behavior.

Be prepared to deal with inappropriate chewing immediately.

Hopefully the issue will not arise, but you should correct destructive behavior as soon as it happens. If your dog chews on a piece of furniture, for example, try placing a strip of double sided tape at the spot where your dog sunk his or her teeth in. When your dog encounters the sticky tape, he or she will hopefully back off right away, deterred by the uncomfortable feeling. Other options include bitter apple spray or lemon rind to repel your dog's interest. You can also offer your dog an appropriate item like a bully stick to chew on instead.

Make a bad weather plan.

If you and your dog are used to going out at lunch for a walk and potty break, you may want to think of an alternate idea in case of inclement weather. Rain or snow may not be problematic at home for quick bathroom trips, but at work you may not be able to deal with damp clothing, soggy shoes, and the dreaded wet dog smell. Consider having your dog use a potty pad in the bathroom or even in a parking garage. Scout the building for exits with potential cover from stormy weather. Keep an umbrella nearby. Consider using both person sized and doggy sized raincoats and boots.

Have a lighted collar or leash ready if needed.

If you come or go from your workplace in darkness, consider outfitting your dog with a lighted collar. Visibility is an important aspect of your dog's safety. The increased visibility of a lighted collar or leash can be very helpful when walking through streets or parking lots where drivers aren't expecting to encounter a dog.

Consider using a dog-safe air or fabric freshener.

It may be beneficial to spray a deodorizer or air freshener in your workplace at the end of the day, especially if your work space has carpets or soft furnishings. It will keep your workplace smelling fresh and remove any dog related odors. By using the product at the end of the day, the air freshener can filter around the space without bothering any humans or dogs, making the room fresh when you arrive the next day.

Check your dog over at the end of each day.

It's very easy for a dropped staple or paper clip to get stuck in your dog's paws or fur. At the end of the day, give your dog a quick rub down. Your dog will enjoy a nice massage while you feel for any abnormalities in your dog's fur / skin / paws /mouth, etc. If you notice your dog limping or constantly licking or scratching a certain area, inspect that spot thoroughly.

Be considerate.

Not everyone is a dog lover. You may find that there are some people at your workplace that do not appreciate having an animal around. There may also encounter people suffering from allergies. Make sure your dog is polite and respects the boundaries set by others. Don't let your dog try to force interaction from those unwilling or unable to give attention to a dog.

Conclusion

Learn to trust your instincts. No one knows your dog better than you. If your dog enjoys spending the day at work with you, great. But it's also okay if your dog seems happier at home. Maybe your dog needs more time to get used to new situations. Maybe it's better to alternate days where your dog stays home with days where your dog goes to work. Just pay attention to your dog's body language and demeanor to help you figure out the right plan for you and your specific dog.

If you are a conscientious and responsible dog owner, then there is every chance that you and your dog will enjoy a successful working relationship. Be prepared to react, correct, or take responsibility for your dog whenever necessary. As long as work gets done with minimal disruptions, your work days can be much more enjoyable with your canine companion by your side.

<u>Workplace Checklist</u>

Below is a checklist of items that I have mentioned using in this book. Use this list as a helpful tool to decide if you have everything you plan to bring to your workplace for your dog.

- ☐ Food
- ☐ Treats
- ☐ Airtight food container(s)
- ☐ Dog bed(s)
- ☐ Blanket
- ☐ Towel(s)
- ☐ Water bowl
- ☐ Food bowl (or slow feeder bowl)
- ☐ Collapsible bowls
- ☐ Bottled water
- ☐ Placemat
- ☐ Poop bags
- ☐ Potty pads

☐ Crate / playpen / baby gate

☐ Rug(s)

Cleaning supplies:
☐ disinfectant wipes
☐ spot cleaner
☐ paper towels
☐ Air freshener / room deodorizing spray
☐ Hand sanitizer
☐ Wet wipes

☐ Comb / brush

☐ Lint roller

☐ Toys

☐ Dog chews

☐ Treat dispenser or puzzle

☐ Extra collar / leash / harness

☐ ID tag with work address / phone number

☐ Lighted collar / leash

☐ Storage for dog supplies

☐ Business card from your veterinarian

☐ Vaccination records / certificate

☐ Sign warning of your dog's presence

☐ Pet rescue window decal for emergency responders

☐ List of foods harmful to dogs

Bad weather gear:
☐ Umbrella
☐ Human and/or dog raincoat
☐ Human and/or dog boots

☐ _____

☐ _____

☐ _____

☐ _____

☐ _____

☐ _____

☐ _____

☐ _____

Don't Miss These Other Great Books!

How To Get Your Dog To Eat
by Mary DiTosto

25 Reasons Your Dog Isn't Eating

by Mary DiTosto

101 Tips for
Terrific Trips with Your Dog.

by Mary DiTosto

Halloween Costume Cuteness:
How To Choose the Right
Halloween Costume for Your Dog

by Mary DiTosto

About the Author

Mary DiTosto is the proud Dog Mom to a very picky Yorkipoo named Sadie. You can follow all of Sadie's adventures and see all of her adorable photos on her dog blog at http://yourdesignerdogblog.com.

YourDesignerDogBlog.com

Visit us on social media – we'd love to hear from you!

http://www.instagram.com/yourdesignerdog

http://www.twitter.com/yourdesignerdog

http://www.facebook.com/yourdesignerdog

http://www.pinterest.com/yourdesignerdog

www.ingramcontent.com/pod-product-compliance
Lightning Source LLC
Chambersburg PA
CBHW072254170526
45158CB00003BA/1072